CELLO

Movie and TV Music

The Avengers..2

Captain America March.................................3

Doctor Who XI...4

Downton Abbey 5

Game of Thrones 6

Guardians of the Galaxy 7

Hawaii Five-O Theme 8

Married Life (from *UP*) 9

Outlander Theme (The Skye Boat Song)......10

Prologue and Prologue Part 2 (from *Beauty and the Beast*) 11

Rey's Theme (from *Star Wars: The Force Awakens*)...................12

Test Drive (from *How to Train Your Dragon*) 16

Theme from The X-Files...14

Audio Arrangements by Peter Deneff

To access audio visit:
www.halleonard.com/mylibrary

Enter Code
5039-4715-5663-4671

ISBN 978-1-5400-2071-0

HAL•LEONARD®

Visit Hal Leonard Online at
www.halleonard.com

Contact Us:
Hal Leonard
7777 West Bluemound Road
Milwaukee, WI 53213
Email: info@halleonard.com

In Europe contact:
Hal Leonard Europe Limited
Distribution Centre, Newmarket Road
Bury St Edmunds, Suffolk, IP33 3YB
Email: info@halleonardeurope.com

In Australia contact:
Hal Leonard Australia Pty. Ltd.
4 Lentara Court
Cheltenham, Victoria, 3192 Australia
Email: info@halleonard.com.au

THE AVENGERS
from THE AVENGERS

CELLO

Composed by
ALAN SILVESTRI

CAPTAIN AMERICA MARCH

from CAPTAIN AMERICA

CELLO

By ALAN SILVESTRI

DOCTOR WHO XI

CELLO

By MURRAY GOLD

DOWNTON ABBEY
(Theme)

CELLO

Music by JOHN LUNN

GAME OF THRONES

Theme from the HBO Series GAME OF THRONES

By RAMIN DJAWADI

CELLO

GUARDIANS OF THE GALAXY

from GUARDIANS OF THE GALAXY

CELLO

Composed by TYLER BATES,
DIETER HARTMANN, TIMOTHY WILLIAMS
and KURT OLDMAN

HAWAII FIVE-O THEME

from the Television Series

CELLO

By MORT STEVENS

MARRIED LIFE

from UP

By MICHAEL GIACCHINO

CELLO

OUTLANDER THEME
(The Skye Boat Song)

CELLO

Traditional Music
Arranged by BEAR McCREARY

PROLOGUE AND PROLOGUE PART 2

from BEAUTY AND THE BEAST

Cello

REY'S THEME
from STAR WARS: THE FORCE AWAKENS

CELLO

Music by JOHN WILLIAMS

THEME FROM THE X-FILES

from the Twentieth Century Fox Television Series THE X-FILES

CELLO

By MARK SNOW

TEST DRIVE
from the Motion Picture HOW TO TRAIN YOUR DRAGON

CELLO

By JOHN POWELL